Amsterdam: Made by Hand

AMSTERDAM: MADE BY HAND

Pia Jane Bijkerk

THE LITTLE BOOKROOM

New York

Text ©2010 Pia Jane Bijkerk
Photographs ©2010 Pia Jane Bijkerk

Cover design and photograph: Pia Jane Bijkerk
Interior based on a design by Laura Jane Coats
Production: Adam Hess

Bijkerk, Pia.
 Amsterdam : made by hand / by Pia Jane Bijkerk.
     p. cm.
 Includes index.
 ISBN 978-1-892145-84-0 (alk. paper)
 1. Handicraft—Netherlands—Amsterdam—Guidebooks.
 2. Artisans—Netherlands—Amsterdam—Guidebooks.
 3. Shopping—Netherlands—Amsterdam—Guidebooks. I. Title.
 TT78.A48B56 2010
 745.09492'352--dc22

                        2009051941

Published by The Little Bookroom
435 Hudson St., 3rd floor
New York NY 10014
www.littlebookroom.com
editorial@littlebookroom.com

10 9 8 7 6 5 4 3 2 1

Printed in the United States of America

CONTENTS

———◆———

✦

MANY YEARS AGO I HAD A VIVID DREAM ABOUT A CITY MADE UP OF ISLANDS WITH CLUSTERS OF CREATIVE PEOPLE. THERE WERE ARTI-sans, artists, and designers hidden in backstreet studios, tucked away inside beautiful old buildings, making interesting objects with their hands, and their creative energy enlivened the streets. I woke up feeling full of excitement and hope. Could a place like this really exist?

In the autumn of 2007 I moved to Amsterdam where, during each visit over the previous decade, I had always been enamored with the charming architecture of the canal houses, the watery surroundings, and the old-worldliness that emanates from every nook and cranny. Then, just the other day, while exploring my village-like city, and searching out the best-kept "made by hand" secrets for this book, I was taking a moment of rest on a canal bridge, breathing in the picturesque scenery. As I looked around, I realized that this unique place, divided as it is by a multitude of canals and bordered by polders, has the sense of being like a series of islands, overflowing with artists and artisans, abundant and flourishing, yet often out of sight from the main thoroughfares. As I took another breath, my dream from years ago came flooding back and there it stood in front of me, as vibrant and real as a dream could ever be.

It is with the greatest pleasure that I have written my second *Made by Hand* book about Amsterdam. This city that I now call home is bursting with creativity. It's a city that has always thrived on innovation and inspiration, even in its earliest days when trading was its mainstay. Back then, sailors brought gifts of beautiful cloth from faraway lands. These fabrics were stitched into traditional garments and, the designs are still a source of inspiration today as you will soon discover in the pages that follow.

In more modern times, Amsterdam and the Netherlands have become well known internationally for exceptional design. Although it has become more difficult to find people who work with their hands, crafting their own designs, they are here—concealed all the more by recent trends, yet as alive and active as ever—stitching, soldering, hammering, sanding, and working on new ideas all the while. This book is an insider's look into Amsterdam's artisans and handmade specialty boutiques.

Among the pages of this guide you will discover a boutique that has been selling items made by local craftswomen for more than one hundred years, and a bookstore that only sells books made by artists. There is an interior decorator whose antique-filled atelier is a place I visit regularly for sourcing interesting objects for photo shoots (not to mention ideas), and a tiny letterpress studio where I have invitations and cards made. There are jewelers, dressmakers, ceramicists, furniture restorers, a soap maker, a hatmaker, a button collector, and an upholsterer, all of them nestled into the charming streets of the city, across bridges and between canals.

One of the most beguiling characteristics of Amsterdam's creative scene is the unique ability to incorporate the old with the new—not just materials, but techniques and styles. Somehow the style of the seventeenth century mixes seamlessly with the twenty-first century, and all centuries in between. Yet Amsterdam remains one of the most design-forward cities in the world, with the future always in its sights even though there is an air of the found, restored, re-invented, and rescued. Because of this, it's not easy to describe the style of the city, but if I were to give it a try, I would use the words quaint, industrial, charismatic, and bold. Contradictory? Perhaps, but this is a creative hive that has no boundaries or bias. It's a city that welcomes newcomers and cultivates ingenuity.

Amsterdam is a wonderful example of creative people seeking out creative places. For this reason you will find pockets of ateliers around the city. Old, abandoned warehouses are turned into thriving "artist's nests," and entire streets become artistic enclaves all to themselves. It makes the act of discovering these places on your own such a thrill, one I hope to pass to you with this book, not by creating an exhaustive guide but, instead, a strategically selective one—a guide that will open your eyes and mind to all things handmade, one that will steer you toward your own unique finds along the way. Create your own map: the key is to step off the beaten track and head down quaint little streets that look quiet but alluring in some way, for some reason yet unknown to you.

Markets are also a big part of Amsterdam's creative scene. Local artists and craftspeople, boutique owners and bargain hunters, all on the lookout for something special, frequent these unique open-air markets that are sprinkled around the city. While I've included the Noordermarkt (page 30), I also urge you to check out the Sunday Market Amsterdam (www.sundaymarketamsterdam.com), which is held four times a year and features a fabulous group of local artisans selling their latest creations. In summer you can wander through the market while indulging in homemade crêpes and listening to a Cuban band, and in winter sip mulled wine and warm yourself over the open fires to keep cosy while you browse the stalls which line the waterway.

Three years ago, my partner and I had the luck of finding a small houseboat, which we still call home. It is moored on a canal street lined with chestnut trees, and the sunlight dances through the leaves and onto the narrow, cobblestone path. Regal street lamps, some even topped with miniature iron crowns, light up at dusk, and an antiquated, weathered sign that says "atelier" swings gently in the breeze above one of the old doorways in the neighborhood. There are art galleries and private studios with big open windows dotted along the way. After moving into our houseboat I discovered serendipitously, that, once upon a time, it was used as a ceramics studio. It's proof that creativity pops up in the most unexpected places, and discovering them unlocks this wondrous city's best-kept secrets. This is what Amsterdam is all about.

—PIA JANE BIJKERK

Amsterdam, January 2010

WANDER

Haarlemmerdijk

WANDER

1

WHEN TRAVELERS ARRIVE IN AMSTERDAM, THEIR ARRIVAL POINT IS MORE OFTEN THAN NOT THE 120-YEAR-OLD CENTRAAL TRAIN station, an awe-inspiring and majestic structure. The next part of the journey is usually a walk down the central street of Amsterdam called the Damrak, a thoroughfare packed with tourist shops and not-so-enticing cafés, a far cry from the grand edifice they just left. Instead of heading down the Damrak, I suggest you turn right, toward the west, where your first impressions of this enchanting city will be just what you imagined—little cobblestone streets lined with quirky canal houses and pretty bridges. Here is the beginning of the Jordaan, an area that Amsterdammers cherish. You'll find dozens of quaint specialty shops, bustling cafés filled with locals, cool and casual bars and, yes, artists and artisans galore. Our first handmade port of call? The hip, happening Haarlemmerdijk. While on this wander, stop off for a tea break at the popular Tea Bar (Haarlemmerdijk 71) and choose from more than a hundred different types of tea, then head around the corner to the ever-lively Small World café (Binnenoranjestraat 14) for a bite to eat. The seating is minimal with only a few outdoor stools, but the food is fabulous and the atmosphere encapsulates the real city vibe: welcome to Amsterdam.

RESTORED

Haarlemmerdijk 39
TELEPHONE + 31 (0)20 3376473
Monday through Friday + 10:00 am to 6:00 pm
Saturday + 11:00 am to 5:00 pm
www.restored.nl

＊

RESTORED IS HARDLY MORE THAN A YEAR OLD AND AL-READY IT'S GETTING REGULAR ATTENTION FROM LOCAL press, shelter magazines, and stylists who adore the ambient space and curious collection of handmade wares that reflects the aesthetic of owners Marijke Hukema and Petra van der Scheer.

The stunning original art deco window is an ideal frame and viewing point into the store from the busy street. Every month or so, owners Marijke and Petra transform the window display into an imaginative work of art, using new stock as inspiration. Inside the shop, the dark charcoal gray wall is hung with cleverly affixed secondhand cabinets that, along with side tables painted the same striking color, provide a dramatic backdrop for vignettes.

The boutique showcases the owners' own work, along with that of other designers, many of whom use recycled material in innovative ways. For example, dainty teacups are reinvented as wine glasses and fastened by thin glass pedestals to small plates that are ideal for holding nibbles at your next party. Vintage porcelain saucers are drilled with tiny holes to become soap dishes; plain Japanese paper lanterns are

fitted with specially-made fabric covers; stylish handbags are fashioned from recycled fabrics; plain cushion covers are embellished with detailed hand-embroidery; the list goes on. Prices start at 5€. Themed workshops with different designers are held regularly in-store and are listed on the website.

VIVIAN HANN

Haarlemmerdijk 102
TELEPHONE + 31 (0)6 22049465
Tuesday through Friday + 11:00 am to 6:00 pm
Saturday + 10:30 am to 5:00 pm

V IVIAN HANN SELLS QUALITY EUROPEAN CERAMICS HERE FROM HER BOUTIQUE ON THE HISTORIC HARLEMMERDIJK, and in ten years has established an international customer base.

While she stocks many high-end brands, it's her eye for beautiful made-by-hand ceramics that first caught my eye when a friend brought me to the store some years back. Vivien has a rotating selection of pieces from local ceramicists, including Margti Seland, Jas/MW, and Marie Raab, who infuse materials such as gold and glass into their pieces. Vivian, who comes from a background in industrial design, appreciates the technical knowledge of artisans who have spent years perfecting their craft, but her selection process is intuitive: she feels that objects should make you feel happy when you look at them. She is first drawn to the material used, whether it is wood, porcelain, shell, or silver; she then turns her attention to the skill and craftsmanship.

Cutlery is also a significant part of the store's stock, and Vivian is known for stocking the famed flatware of cutlery manufacturer Hugo Pott. Every piece is hand-produced in

Germany; this shop has one of the largest collections of Pott flatware in the Netherlands.

The boutique is informal yet with a sophisticated touch, as visually soothing as the unique and innovative tableware Vivian sells. Prices start at 5€ for porcelain spoons, with small handmade cups, vases, and bowls averaging around 35€.

TYPIQUE

Haarlemmerdijk 123
TELEPHONE + 31 (0)20 6222146
Monday through Saturday ◆ 10:00 am to 6:00 pm
www.typique.nl

◆

THIS SOMEWHAT DIMINUTIVE SHOPFRONT CONCEALS THE SCOPE AND CREATIVITY OF THE WORK THAT TAKES PLACE in the adjoining spaces of this rather wonderful typography boutique. For thirty years owner René Treumann has been designing and printing posters, birth announcements, wedding invitations, artwork, and greeting cards "the old-fashioned way" here in his boutique-atelier.

After graduating from the Rietveld Academy with a degree in typography in the late sixties, René started a small letterpress business with two other specialty printers. As the letterpress process began to be replaced by more modern technologies, they collected discarded equipment and type from larger print houses. After a decade, René opened his own shop, and has been there ever since, creating beautiful handset print work. Many of the motifs are his designs, cut from vinyl. Hundreds of drawers and shelves contain his extensive selection of antique wood print blocks, some with type, some with images. Each drawer is labeled by theme, such as boats, hands, windmills, decorative lines, flora, farm animals, and so on.

Even though this is primarily a shop for locals who come

here for custom work, René also prints and designs an impressive array of postcards, cards, and limited edition prints for the passing trade. Every now and then he creates a body of printed artwork that he exhibits on the white wood-paneled walls of his boutique. "Building Castles in the Air" was a recent exhibition; the original prints sell for 450€ each. Postcards and cards sell from 1€ to 3€, and custom orders start at around 40€.

WANDER

Noordermarkt

WANDER

2

THE NOORDERMARKT IS ONE OF AMSTERDAM'S MOST POPULAR MARKETS, HELD EVERY SATURDAY AND MONDAY OUTSIDE THE Noorderkerk (the "northern church"). I go there all the time, and I've bought all sorts of things, from vintage ribbon, buttons, and a beautiful old rattan chest, to old photos (I used the frames of some of them for my photo collage on the front cover of this book). Just the other day I bought a 1920s chandelier and carried it home on my shoulder while riding my bicycle. This is not uncommon in Amsterdam, and it's fun to see people taking home their marketplace finds by bicycle. In this wander I've chosen three stalls to give you a taste of what's inside the market, but don't stop there. Then find a table at Café Winkel to people-watch, rest your weary feet, and indulge in a piece of Dutch apple tart with whipped cream—the line out the front of the café is an indication of how good this pie really is. Later, stroll a little farther south into the charming streets of the Jordaan, then back up along the Prinsengracht and onto the Prinsenstraat and Herenstraat—read the following pages to find out why.

ANNA MARIA PREUß

Noordermarkt
TELEPHONE + 31 (0)20 6223186
Saturday ‹ 9:00 am to 4:00 pm
www.anna.dds.nl

—◆—

ESTLED WITHIN THE HUSTLE AND BUSTLE OF THE ORGANIC PRODUCE SECTION OF THE NOORDERMARKT ON Saturdays, you will find the stall of ceramicist Anna Preuß. Originally from Germany, Anna trained there for three years to learn a special traditional pottery technique. After moving to Amsterdam in 1999, she found a studio and set up her business, selling her earthenware at the Noordermarkt. She enjoys the friendly atmosphere at the market, as well as the diversity. She often paints her bowls, cups, and vases with streetscapes of canal houses; people are welcome to bring in a photo of their neighborhood or favorite canal houses that Anna will use to make a custom piece, which takes between two weeks to a month to complete. Anna's pottery ranges from 11€ for children's bowls and cups up to 150€ for large vases and bowls.

AKELEI

Noordermarkt

TELEPHONE + 31 (0)20 6223186

Saturday • 10:00 am to 4:00 pm ~ Monday • 9:00 am to 1:00 pm

www.akelei.nu

Studio: Van diemenstraat 410

First Thursday of the month • 5:00 pm to 9:00 pm

www.veem.nl

———

ONCE A FULL-TIME INTERIOR ARCHITECT, JEWELRY MAKER AKELEI HERTZBERGER USES A RANGE OF MATERIALS, including stone, porcelain, aluminum, gold, and silver, as well as old found bits and pieces. Her studio, in the beautiful converted warehouse called "het veem" in north Amsterdam, is a treasure trove. There are drawers and drawers of tiny treasures—coral and shells, little plastic toys and broken teacups—amidst the gold, silver, and gemstones that all seem like they have come from the bottom of the ocean, released from a rusted old chest.

Akelei spends her days in her studio, which is perched on the shore of the Ij River, making necklaces, earrings, and rings, and creating custom pieces. For the custom series "stories on a string," she invites customers to bring components (found, inherited, or keepsake) with which she designs one-of-a-kind pieces. The idea is to embody, in a wearable piece of jewelry, the memory of a journey, a love, a birth, or a life. Prices starts at 12€ but vary for custom orders.

ANNE

Noordermarkt
TELEPHONE + 31 (0)20 6223186
Saturday + 9:00 am to 4:00 pm
www.annevandijk.nl

WHEN ANNE VAN DIJK LOOKS AT A BROKEN ZIPPER OR A BICYCLE INNER TUBE—THINGS THAT MOST PEOPLE see as trash—she sees a world of possibilities and opportunities; this vision is the foundation of her small but well-established fashion accessories label.

Anne trained as a painter but felt restricted by traditional materials: instead of painting on canvas, she wanted to paint on old newspaper, and instead of using artists' paint, she wanted to use leftover house paint. Her inclination has always been to use what already exists; so, ten years ago while fixing her bicycle wheel, she cut through the inner tube, felt the material was lovely, and made a bracelet from it. Thus her label began. Now Anne makes, among other things, bags and laptop cases from surplus army tents and secondhand suits; scarves from the sleeves of old jackets and sweaters; and bracelets from zippers. Her studio is packed with fabrics, jackets, ties, and, yes, the odd inner tube. She believes "the solution is always in the material," and cleverly uses existing seams, pockets, and buttonholes to add character to each item.

ROOS SIERAAD

2nd, Anjeliersdwarsstraat 3
TELEPHONE + 31 (0)6 17931826
Monday + 11:00 am to 4:00 pm
Thursday through Saturday + 11:00 am to 6:00 pm

———

THE FIRST TIME I STEPPED INTO ROOS'S BOUTIQUE AND PEERED INTO HER PINEWOOD JEWELRY DISPLAYS, SHE announced from her back-room studio: "Everything here is made by hand by me, I never make the same piece twice, and I often use found objects in my work."

Roos is a confessed bowerbird, collecting trinkets, vintage ornaments, and broken bric-a-brac at *brocantes* in France and local flea markets. She has drawers filled with all sorts of small objects, ready to use as centerpieces for her next work. A recent collection of necklaces used vintage porcelain figurine heads set in silver and attached to crystal beads.

The jewelry made by Roos (simply pronounced "Rose") may seem quite straightforward, but its simplicity is deceptive. Silver tulip shapes that I thought were meant to dangle from the earlobe are actually much more complex. When Roos showed me how to wear the earrings, I realized they were carefully designed to sit neatly against the ear while, unusually, long studs dangled behind the lobe. And what at first looked like metal mesh is actually handmade silver thread knitted by Roos into complex weaves that she then fashions into earrings, bracelets, and neckpieces. Pieces start at 14€.

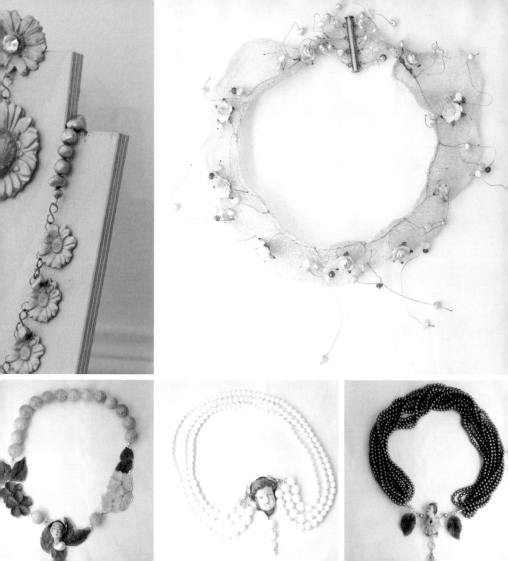

ILV

Prinsengracht 201
TELEPHONE + 31 (0)40 2693032
Monday through Friday + 9:30 am to 6:00 pm
Saturday + 11:00 am to 5:00 pm
www.ilovevintage.nl

WHEN I FIRST SPOTTED ILV ("ILOVEVINTAGE"), IT WAS LOCATED ON THE EVER-ENCHANTING HERENSTRAAT, JUST off the Heren canal. I was delightfully surprised to find this new little temporary boutique that exuded charm and style, filled with pretty vintage frocks, shoes, and handmade jewelry.

Run by brother and sister Babak and Faranak Mirjalili, ILV began as an online boutique several years ago when Faranak realized her vintage clothes collection was growing a bit out of control. Her hobby quickly became a business. Soon her friends were hosting "I Love Vintage" evenings to showcase Faranak's fashion finds—just like a modern-day Tupperware party.

Today, the online boutique has grown into a brick-and-mortar shop stocking not only vintage clothing, hats, and shoes, but also limited-edition garments, handmade jewelry, and accessories. The new boutique, located around the corner from the one I first visited, includes an office, atelier, and photography studio. The plan is to create an interactive fashion space where Faranak can host fashion shows, music nights, and workshops where customers will have the opportunity to choose from a handful of designs and have garments made to order.

VAN WEERDE

Herenstraat 17
TELEPHONE + 31 (0)20 6387077
Wednesday through Friday · 11:00 am to 6:00 pm
Saturday · 11:00 am to 5:00 pm

JEROEN VAN WEERDE HAS BEEN RESTORING VINTAGE AND FRENCH ANTIQUE FURNITURE FOR MANY YEARS IN HIS exquisite shop on the quaint Herentraat. He is drawn to simple, rustic farm furniture, without carvings or intricate detailing. The pieces work beautifully with the shop's collection of industrial lamps, 1950s Eames chairs, and antique birdcages. Jeroen finds many of the larger pieces in France. He keeps his eyes peeled for cherry and walnut wood antique furniture, which are among his favorite to restore: "Cherry wood tables with a few hundred years of patina built up, with burns and marks too, have great character," he explains.

He restores the pieces and then displays them with antique books, mirrors, rustic earthenware bowls, wooden ladders, old glassware, and chopping boards. (I have a collection of his chopping boards, which I use repeatedly on food shoots.)

This is a boutique atelier I visit regularly for styling, as I always find something perfect and delightful to photograph. Jeroen has a beautiful eye for simple but functional furniture, and his restoration work is impeccable. Tables range from 600€ to 3000€, birdcages 60€ to 250€, and chopping boards and small items start at 20€.

WANDER

3

Rozengracht

VEZJUN
+ 53 +

SWARM
+ 55 +

WANDER

3

THE ROZENGRACHT IS BETTER KNOWN AS A DESIGN STREET RATHER THAN A HANDMADE DESTINATION. THERE ARE MANY NOTABLE design shops, such as Sprmrkt and Kitsch Kitchen, on this wide road, all within easy strolling distance from each other, but there are also a couple of hidden sources for the handmade worth visiting. To really get a sense of the hip, creative vibe in this neighborhood, check out the very cool Bar Struik (Rozengracht 160), which features a dinner menu by guest cooks that changes daily.

VEZJUN

Rozengracht 110
NO TELEPHONE ~ EMAIL mailto@vezjun.nl
Tuesday, Wednesday & Friday + noon to 7:00 pm
Thursday + noon to 8:00 pm ~ Saturday + 11:00 am to 6:00 pm
www.vezjun.nl

VEZJUN IS A LITTLE BOUTIQUE NESTLED AMONGST BIG DESIGNER HOMEWARES STORES AND FASHION HOUSES. IT'S a sweet shop run by five young local designers making clothes and accessories in limited editions. You will find an eclectic mix that is young, fresh, and daring, with bold colors and interesting fabrics teamed together to make hip and stylish streetwear. Within the collective is Femke Agema's line, pfff, which combines sassy striped and dotted cloth with hints of Indonesian batik in short skirts and pants; she cleverly uses deflated balloons printed with her logo as funky labels. Audrey Weeren's label 3 is a sophisticated range of bags, belts, and accessories made from recycled leather, mostly from discarded couches found on the street; she uses the untouched underside of the material and a stockpile of leather scraps to make new creations. Audrey's bags are around 50€ to 100€ each.

Since the store's inception five years ago, the number of designers involved has grown and changed, and so has the collection, which evolves with seasonal trends and new fabrics. The concept has always remained the same, however: affordable, chic clothes handmade by young Amsterdam designers.

SWARM

Elisabeth Wolffstraat 41 – huis
TELEPHONE + 31 (0)6 44035637
Open by appointment
www.swarmhome.com

——◆——

ALTHOUGH IT IS PRIVATE, I COULD NOT RESIST INCLUDING THIS VERY SPECIAL ATELIER OF LESLIE OSCHMANN, THE former visual director for Anthropologie. After eight years with the company, during the time it expanded from ten stores to more than eighty, Leslie decided it was time to work with her hands. She hopped the Atlantic Ocean to start her new venture. Coming from a visual merchandising background, Leslie likes to work with collections and large groupings; hence the name, Swarm.

Like a few of us expats here, Leslie came to Amsterdam on a whim. Something intangible drew her to this old European city, perhaps the pull of her Dutch heritage combined with an attraction to the creative energy that can be felt as you walk through the streets.

Leslie loved going to European flea markets and, amazed at the number of beautiful old oil paintings for sale, collected masses of them to rework. In her atelier at the back of her apartment, she cuts out pieces within the landscape or portrait and stitches in a silk scarf or vintage paper. When she showed her work to the buyers at Anthropologie, they bought the whole series. Anthropologie became her first customer and today remains one of her biggest, last year buying 125 of her "oil paintings on chairs," a series of chairs with simple lines and wooden backs and seats that she covered in oil paintings.

Each corner of Leslie's home has her distinctive signature, her touch—from curtains held back by beautiful giant wood buckles, to a couch covered in a patchwork of old tartans, to the fireplace pinned with dozens of found portraits. Aesthetically, Leslie is drawn to juxtaposition—shiny with worn, smooth with irregular. She delights in finding new ways to reinvent the use of an object, and her house makes for a wonderful showroom. Although this is her private atelier and home, Leslie is happy for you to come and see her latest work and purchase pieces directly. Her current pieces, the oil painting chairs (200€ to 500€) are dotted throughout the space.

WANDER

Hazenstraat

BR.WN CLOTHES

PETSALON

EVA DAMAVE

WANDER

POETIC, CHARISMATIC, SHORT AND SWEET: THE HAZENSTRAAT IS ONE STREET YOU DO NOT WANT TO MISS WHEN IN AMSTERDAM. IT HAS recently been recognized and officially named the "tenth street"— the famous Nine Streets being just across the Prinsen canal. This is a road for ambling. It's a time-layered, narrow *straat* in the Jordaan packed with boutiques, ateliers, and locals who know just where to go when they want something special. Tucked away from the main canal streets, it is a wonderful example of what Amsterdammers adore about their village-like city. At the end of the street on the corner of the Laurier canal, just before the bridge, you will find The English Bookshop: a perfect literary resting place where, perhaps, you might even find this book.

BR.WN CLOTHES

Hazenstraat 28
TELEPHONE + 31 (0)6 14446089
Thursday & Friday ⋆ noon to 6:00 pm
Saturday ⋆ 12:30 pm to 6:00 pm, and by appointment
www.brownclothes.eu

BRITISH FASHION DESIGNER MELANIE BROWN START-ED HER WOMEN'S FASHION LABEL, BR.WN CLOTHES, IN Amsterdam in 2007 after working for many years as a pattern cutter. She has now opened her first atelier-boutique. Set in a beautiful 1920s storefront with original features, Melanie has created an inviting showroom where buyers can interact with the designer as well as her clothes.

Melanie's latest collection, called "Twice," is about an individual's alter ego, or shadow. Every outfit she has created for the line has an identical version in black, and while the initial piece is made from soft silk to accentuate the silhouette, the black outfit is made from thick cotton to emphasize its form.

Melanie loves creating garments that allow the wearer to interact with the piece. She often lines the opening of a shirt, skirt, or jacket with a long row of buttons so that the wearer can reconfigure a garment and influence its shape. She works with leather as well as silk, sheepskin, fake fur, wool, and cotton; synthetic fabrics are used minimally, for lining purposes. Melanie is happy to make garments to measure and will ship pieces anywhere in the world. Prices for garments range from 20€ to 1200€, with dresses averaging around 200€.

PETSALON

Hazenstraat 3
TELEPHONE + 31 (0)20 6247385
Wednesday through Saturday • noon to 6:00 pm, and by appointment
www.petsalon.nl

—◆—

THE WORD *PET* MEANS "CAP" IN DUTCH. PETSALON IS THE BOUTIQUE AND ATELIER OF LONGTIME HATMAKER ANS Wesseling. For twenty years she has fashioned hats, caps, bonnets, and berets in all sorts of shapes and sizes in felt, leather, wool, linen, and silk. With the exception of the straw hats and felt berets, all hats are made by Ans in her open atelier, separated from the shop by only a bright orange wall filled with handmade hats. Although she is a traditional hat maker, Ans prefers to make casual hats and caps, rather than fancy ones. Her style reflects the vibrant and quirky vibe of the city. If you find a hat you like in her boutique but you feel it needs some adjustments or additions, Ans is happy to make the changes. Prices range from 35€ to 700€.

EVA DAMAVE

2nd Lauriersdwarsstraat 51C

TELEPHONE + 31 (0)20 6277325 or + 31 (0)20 6209318

Wednesday through Saturday · noon to 6:00 pm

www.evadamave.nl

TEXTILE DESIGNER EVA DAMAVE DESCRIBES HER WORK—DESIGNING KNITWEAR—AS IF IT WERE PAINTING ON CANvas: the threads are her colors, her hands are the brushes, and each stroke is a weave. She combines linen, cotton, and wool threads in all different colors to create interesting patterns and then joins each unique pattern to make a patchwork-style garment, cushion, or blanket. The result is a fun, colorful, and imaginative knitwear collection.

Eva has been creating patterns and styles for her knitwear line inside her petite atelier and boutique on this quiet and quaint back street for seventeen years.

Eva often creates double-layered pieces with very fine linen thread. These are made in the city of Tilburg, where she works with craftspeople on specialized weaving machinery. She then combines these weaves with other knits—a garment may be made of sleeves that Eva knits in the Amsterdam studio and front panels that she has made in Tilburg. Sometimes when she cannot quite get the color she wants from one particular thread, she mixes two together, producing yet a new texture and color. Scarves start at 85€, jackets 350€, and blankets 700€.

WANDER

5

De 9 Straatjes (The Nine Streets)

KLEIKOLLEKTIEF

EDDY VAREKAMP

JUFFROUW SPLINTER CURIOSA

LA SAVONNERIE

BOEKIE WOEKIE

DE POSTHUMUSWINKEL

WANDER

D E 9 STRAATJES (THE NINE STREETS) ENCOMPASSES NINE SKINNY STREETS BETWEEN THREE CANALS, FREQUENTED BY LOCALS AND visitors alike. It is a picturesque part of seventeenth-century Amsterdam, with lots of interesting shops on the ground floors of pretty canal houses. The area makes a wonderful day of shopping— there are plenty of cafés, bars, and restaurants where you can rest your feet and people-watch. When I'm in the area, I'm most often found in one of three places: Buffet van Odette (Herengracht 309), Foodware (Looiersgracht 12), or Pancakes!Amsterdam (Berenstraat 38), where, on a cold wintry day, I usually order a lemon and sugar pancake.

In this wander I have chosen six made-by-hand destinations that will take you not only through the Nine Streets but also just a little beyond, giving you a great sense of what this characteristically Amsterdam neighborhood is all about. In spring and summer you will see climbing roses, hollyhocks, and tulips in bloom along the shopfronts, and in autumn and winter the Christmas lights come out and twinkle above as you wander in the romantic mist and semi-darkness. This is a magical part of Amsterdam, and wandering between ateliers and artisan boutiques makes it all the more so.

KLEIKOLLEKTIEF

Hartenstraat 19
TELEPHONE + 31 (0)20 6225727
Wednesday through Saturday • 1:00 pm to 5:00 pm
www.kleikollektief.nl

—◆—

YOU'D BE FORGIVEN IF YOU MISSED THIS SPECIAL BOUTIQUE-ATELIER AS YOU PASS BY ON THE HARTENSTRAAT; KLEI-kollektief ("Clay Collective") is a very narrow space with a small shopfront just big enough for a spray of flowers and a clay pot or two. Inside, though, shelves stretching from floor to ceiling along a long wall display the hand-made creations of two very talented ceramicists, Klaartje Kamermans and Corien Ridderkhoff.

Klaartje and Corien met when they were studying hand-crafts at college. Both experimented with materials such as metal, wood, and paint, but were most inspired by clay. Together they decided to open a ceramics shop and studio in the center of Amsterdam; thirty years later, they are still doing what they love. Corien tends to add geometric patterns to bottles (90€), vases, and bowls (starting at 14€), while Klaartje enjoys working with rounder shapes and softer colors. A rather impressive gas kiln sits at the back of the shop, in the atelier. Klaartje and Corien collaborate with local artists from time to time, including a painter, illustrator, photographer, and textile designer—partnerships that make for an eclectic but cohesive range of pottery, a little something for everybody.

EDDY VAREKAMP

Hartenstraat 30
TELEPHONE + 31 (0)20 6257766 or + 31 (0)6 30250291
Saturday • 1:00 pm to 5:00 pm

❧

EDDY VAREKAMP SPECIALIZES IN LINO PRINTING AND HAS A WONDERFUL STUDIO IN THE JORDAAN WHICH LOOKS small from the outside, but opens up into a seemingly never-ending series of rooms filled with drawers of specialty papers, lino, carving equipment, brushes, woodblocks, and hand-printing paraphernalia. His boutique gallery is a short bike ride away from his studio and is nestled within the Nine Streets on the Hartenstraat.

Walls and simple wooden art racks neatly display Eddy's diverse assortment of hand-printed artwork. From time to time he collaborates with local ceramicists to make bowls, vases, and plates that carry his distinctive painting style; they are also on display in the boutique. Some of my favorites of his prints are the Amsterdam street scenes depicting the lively village-like streets complete with lopsided canal houses, boats, and bikes.

Postcards are 5€ and prints anywhere from 20€ to 500€.

JUFFROUW SPLINTER CURIOSA

Prinsengracht 230
TELEPHONE + 31 (0)20 3305515
Monday + 1:00 pm to 6:00 pm
Tuesday through Friday + 11:00 am to 6:00 pm
Saturday + 11:00 am to 5:00 pm
(Sunday in summer, check website for hours)
www.juffrouwsplinter.nl

❖

JUFFROUW SPLINTER CURIOSA WAS THE FIRST BOUTIQUE I
FELL IN LOVE WITH IN AMSTERDAM. I WAS CAPTIVATED BY
everything from the French fisherman chairs outside,
with their chipped-paint wood slats, to the alluring window
display full of vintage finds that hinted at what was awaiting
inside: European biscuit tins (3€ to 10€), glass bottles (6€)
and dainty lanterns, enamelware, china, and lots of skillfully
restored secondhand furniture (very well priced at 50€ to
500€).

Owner Jolijn Bosma's love of old and pretty homewares, as
well as the pleasure she takes in refurbishing found furniture
and market buys, inspired her to set up shop about seven
years ago, here on the edge of the famous Nine Streets. Her
store is frequented by many interior stylists, visual mer-
chandisers, and set dressers, not just for the ever-changing
collection but also for inspiration. The way Jolijn displays
her stock ignites the imagination of her customers, and she
is more than happy for people to replicate her ideas with
their new purchases in their own homes.

Jolijn often works with stylists to create unique pieces for photo shoots. On one occasion, food and interior stylist Cyn Fernandus bought a number of Jolijn's vintage plates to make into five-tiered cake stands for a magazine spread, which were then sold in the boutique. Cyn has continued to make exclusive items for Jolijn, including a collection of classic lampshades that were outdated until she refashioned them with collectible stamps. The lampshades are perched on old lamp bases giving the lamps a fresh, fun new look that reminds me of the bright and bold colors of Cuba (49.95€ each).

This is a boutique I come to often to find treasures for both my work and my home. I often bike past with no intention of stopping—but then something in the window catches my eye and I find myself inside. After a quick chat with Jolijn and a parcel under my arm, I step out smiling and continue riding down the Prinsengracht.

LA SAVONNERIE

Prinsengracht 294
TELEPHONE + 31 (0)20 4281139
Monday through Saturday ♦ 10:00 am to 6:00 pm
occasionally on Sunday, depending on the weather
www.savonnerie.nl

THIS LITTLE SOAP-MAKING BOUTIQUE IS THE ONLY SHOP OF ITS KIND IN THE NETHERLANDS. IT STOCKS THE KIND OF handmade soaps that you would expect to find in the country markets of France. Indeed, they seem so authentically French that they are used regularly by stylists and editors of French magazines as well as other high-profile lifestyle publications around the globe.

The soaps sold by owner Turid Nilsen come in all sorts of shapes, scents, and sizes; ingredients are 100% vegetable, have no added chemicals, preservatives, or parabens, and are not tested on animals. The shop also has an appealing selection of other European products to choose from, such as exfoliants and body creams, handmade brushes, ceramic dishes, toiletry bags, and towels. Turid and her team also fill custom orders; names and logos can be stamped into any bars of soap. The soap is made in 5 kg batches, so large orders need to be placed several months in advance, especially at Christmas. However, some personalized orders can be filled in just a couple of days; pop in or call for details. The soaps cost from 3€ to 10€, with the popular 25gm alphabet block soaps just 90 cents each.

LAVANDE

BOEKIE WOEKIE

Berenstraat 16
TELEPHONE + 31 (0)20 6390507
Daily + noon to 6:00 pm
www.boekiewoekie.com

◆

AMSTERDAM IS A CITY OF ART. ON ALMOST EVERY STREET AND AROUND ALMOST EVERY CORNER THERE SEEM TO BE artists' studios, galleries, and open-air sculptures by artists and of artists. There are art markets, as well as open atelier weekends, year-round. There have been thousands of books over the centuries written about the artists who have lived and passed through Amsterdam, but what about books actually made by the artists themselves? Boekie Woekie is a unique and unassuming space that sells these very special publications. Here, you will be able to hold in your hand intimate works by artists from far and wide—some in small print runs, and others unique editions bound individually by hand.

In Dutch, the name Boekie Woekie (pronounce "boogie woogie") translates as "shaky business," and the founders, book artists themselves, thought that was exactly what their "business" would be—uncertain and unsteady. Amsterdam, however, thriving as it is with artists and travelers, embraced Boekie Woekie; today, twenty-three years later, the shop stocks more than 8,000 titles.

Here you will find unusual and unexpected books. Some have

hand-drawn or hand-painted pictures and stories in many different languages; there are diaries and journals that you would never see elsewhere.

This is a shop in which to linger and browse. At the very least, if you don't find a book that "speaks" to you, you may find something in the wide selection of artists' postcards. Check out the revolving card stand near the desk with the handwritten sign saying "boekie woekie cleaners"—these are old found postcards that have been scrunched up, washed by hand, and then ironed out to form completely reinvented postcards.

DE POSTHUMUSWINKEL

Sint Luciënsteeg 23-25
TELEPHONE + 31 (0)20 6255812
Monday → noon to 5:00 pm
Tuesday through Friday → 9:00 am to 5:00 pm
Saturday → 11:00 am to 5:00 pm
www.posthumuswinkel.nl

◆

ET IN ONE OF THE MOST HISTORIC PARTS OF THE CITY CEN-
TER IS THE ROYAL POSTHUMUSWINKEL, A *WINKEL* (SHOP)
that has been making and selling custom-made stamps
of every kind since 1865. The store is a landmark for lovers
of stationery and hand-printing supplies. You can find not
only a seemingly limitless array of stamps, but also beautiful
paper, envelopes, old-fashioned shop tags strung with twine,
and inks of all colors and types. The store is somewhat of
a museum, too, with antique letters with embossed letter-
heads and monograms, glass wax stamps, antique printing
machines, and old photographs of the store on display. It
is easy to imagine people visiting the store more than 140
years ago, as the original architectural details are still very
much a part of the present. The time-layered ambience gives
a lovely sense of nostalgia, but the diverse stock accom-
modates modern times. Current owners Peter and Nathalie
Breurken took the business over from Peter's father a few
years ago, who took over along with two of Peter's uncles
from their father before that.

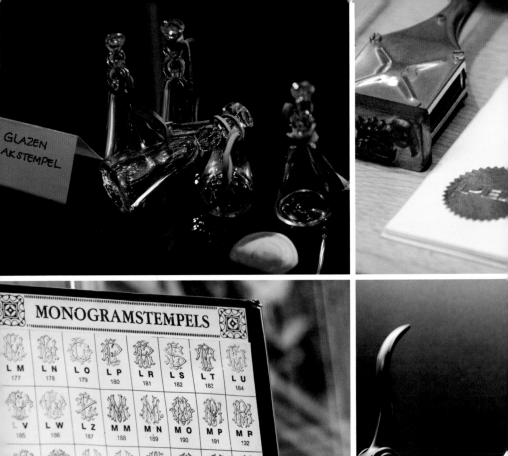
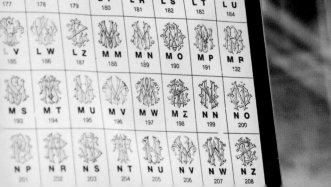

De heer en m...
Th. van de Westl...
genoegen u kenn...
het vernemen ...
Mischa in het h...
met Mar... ...

...trouwen...
30 uur.
...Kerp. He...
...kerdam.

INZEGENING VAN HET HUWELIJK VAN

MANON VAN LYNDEN

&

WANDER

6

Nieuwe Kerk

GILD GOLDSMITH ATELIER

DEN HAAN & WAGENMAKERS BV – DUTCH QUILTS

WANDER

6

IN BETWEEN THE NINE STREETS AND THE RED LIGHT DISTRICT, JUST A STONE'S THROW NORTH AND FACING DAM SQUARE, IS THE NIEUWE Kerk. *Nieuwe kerk*, which means "new church," is, in fact, very old. Dating back to the fifteenth century, this cathedral today stands rather somberly with its gothic towers and dark roof structure. If you walk around the back of the building, you will discover some tiny boutiques, bars, and cafés tucked into the nooks and crannies of the neighborhood's skinny houses, as well as a couple of not-to-be-missed places to find handmade treasures. Depending on how much walking you feel like doing on one day, this is a wander to continue on from the preceding and/or subsequent one. While you're here, take rest at Café Belgique (Gravenstraat 2), one of Amsterdam's smallest bars, packed with charm and a great mix of locals, or stop by for a delicious cupcake at De Drie Graefjes (The Three Little Dukes, Eggertstraat 1).

GILD GOLDSMITH ATELIER

Eggertstraat 2
TELEPHONE + 31 (0)20 4210093
Monday • 11:00 am to 5:00 pm
Tuesday through Saturday • 11:00 am to 6:00 pm
Sunday • noon to 5:00 pm
www.gildgold.com

GILD IS ONE OF THOSE ENCHANTING ATELIER-BOUTIQUES THAT YOU HOPE TO STUMBLE UPON WHEN WANDERING the streets of any city. In fact, when I first stumbled upon Gild, I thought a little magic was in play because I was very sure it was not there the last time I walked down the cobbled path out front. I was right—although it looks as if it's always been there, Gild Atelier is only a year old. It has caught not only my eye, but also those of other passersby who are drawn to the stunning jewelry displayed in antique glass domes in the windows that suggest dozens of looking glasses inviting a peek into a different world.

Fraukje Teppema is the young jeweler working behind the window lined with clamps, tweezers, files, and pliers. She lives in the neighborhood, and when she saw this empty miniscule space, she thought it presented a wonderful opportunity to set up her first boutique, selling not only her latest pieces but also those of other jewelry artists whose work she likes.

Fraukje's pieces are contemporary, sometimes bold, often textural, and always timeless. She manages to create things for a variety of tastes, not only by her use of different metals and jewels (such as diamonds, pearls, smoky quartz, and sapphires), but by the range of prices as well. Her pieces start at as little as 20€, and slowly work their way up to 500€. Even though the variety is wide, the collection is unified. The strong narrative comes from Fraukje's stylish and sophisticated aesthetic and her impeccable craftsmanship.

DEN HAAN & WAGENMAKERS BV DUTCH QUILTS

Nieuwezijds Voorburgwal 97-99
TELEPHONE + 31 (0)20 6202525
Tuesday through Saturday ✦ 10:00 am to 5:00 pm
www.dutchquilts.com

O N THE CORNER OF SINT NICOLAASSTRAAT AND THE ALMOST UNPRONOUNCEABLE NIEUWEZIJDS VOORBURGWAL IS A little set of stone stairs with a traditional Dutch door at the landing. As you open the door and step inside, you will find an unusually shaped old-fashioned room swathed from floor to ceiling in seemingly every style of Dutch quilting fabric available. This is the retail headquarters for the world-renowned Dutch reproduction fabric company Den Haan & Wagenmakers BV, more familiarly known in English simply as Dutch Quilts. Recently handed over to new owners Petra Prins and Nel Kooiman, Dutch Quilts has been in business for twenty-five years, showcasing a vast collection of cotton chintzes based on original hand-printed designs that were brought to Dutch shores by the East India Company during the seventeenth century.

The original designs were primarily used in the Netherlands for interior furnishings such as cushion covers, drapes, and wall coverings, as well as for national costumes. In the 1700s, the floral cotton chintzes became popular for clothing. Today, the designs are widely used by quilters and fabric enthusiasts around the world. This is a treasure chest for illustrators, color consultants, fashion designers, and decorators as well.

Within the boutique are all sorts of examples of how the fabric can be used, from a number of patchwork quilts in varying colorways hanging from balustrades, doors, and hooks, to curtains, stitched ornaments, and traditional garments, as well as a dramatic floor-to-ceiling wall covering that lines the front windows (look behind you as you first enter the space). Upstairs are dozens of boxes filled with fabric bundles in hundreds of colors and designs, carefully arranged and beautifully styled. The fabrics themselves beckon to be touched and viewed up close. There is a wall of American patchwork fabrics as well, giving the local clientele an immense selection from which to choose.

The fabrics are priced from 22€ to 35€ per meter and are sold in small or large quantities, depending on your needs.

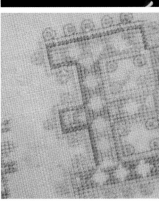

W A N D E R

7

Nieuwmarkt

WANDER

7

TWO OF MY FAVORITE TEXTILE BOUTIQUES ARE IN THE NIEUWMARKT AREA OF AMSTERDAM. ONE SELLS LUSCIOUS SILKS AND HANDWOVEN natural fabrics; the other, cotton, bamboo, wool, silk, and velvet, screen-printed and plant-dyed in the studio attached to the boutique. While you wander between the two, take in the sights around you— this is a very old part of Amsterdam, dating back to the 1400s. Wander down along the canal Kloveniersburgwal toward Staalstraat, a quaint shopping street filled with boutiques selling vintage clothing, book-stores, cafés, and the famous design house Droog. There may be only two made-by-hand destinations on this little wander, but it is still a wonderfully atmospheric place to be. You can buy some hand-dipped chocolates at Puccini Bomboni (Staalstraat 17), or rest in the adjacent café and enjoy lunch or a delicious hot chocolate, a favorite Saturday afternoon treat for me. If you feel like walking some more, head over the bridge to the Waterlooplein markets, open every day except Sunday. Here, I often find something old-fashioned and uniquely Dutch to slip into my shopping basket, a much better souvenir than the mass-produced touristy items found in droves on the main streets.

CAPSICUM NATUURSTOFFEN

Oude Hoogstraat 1
TELEPHONE + 31 (0)20 6231016
Monday + 11:00 am to 6:00 pm
Tuesday through Saturday + 10:00 am to 6:00 pm
Sunday + 1:00 pm to 5:00 pm
www.capsicum.nl

◆

Inside this beautifully designed boutique is every color of silk you could ever wish for, alongside reams of hand-embroidered cotton, handwoven scarves, bedspreads, cushions, throws, tablecloths, and napkins…have I missed anything? No doubt I have—this is a boutique that you have to see with your own eyes in order to comprehend the range of textiles offered.

Everything in Capsicum is crafted from natural fabrics and made by hand. The creative team works closely with weavers in India to produce exclusive designs and patterns each year. This is not a textile company that follows seasonal trends; instead, the designers aim for timeless fabrics and impeccable quality. Nelleke van de Streek is the new owner, having recently taken over the thirty-five-year-old business from the original owners Steve and Deborah Pepper (hence the clever store name). Regular clients include interior decorators, costume designers, and stylists who come to select fabrics for magazine shoots. Fabric pieces as small as 25 cm may be purchased. Prices start at around 17€ per meter for various cottons, with silks averaging 45€ per meter. There are plenty of readymade cushions, as well as other home furnishings, for 25€ to 40€.

CAPSICUM®
NATUURSTOFFEN

CODE Kussens Brocade
MATERIAAL zijde/viscose
OORSPRONG india
BREEDTE 40 x40
PRYS € 37.50

met vulling

TINCTORIA

Zanddwarsstraat 9
TELEPHONE + 31 (0)20 6238008
MOBILE + 31 (0)6 15006956
Monday through Friday • 10:00 am to 6:00 pm (best to call first)
www.tinctoria.nl

FOLLOW THE CHIMING ZUIDERKERK BELLS TO FIND THIS LITTLE GEM, TUCKED AWAY ON A SMALL NARROW STREET right under the church steeple. Tinctoria may look like a sweet little shopfront with blue wooden window frames, but there is more here than meets the eye. In what was formerly a stable, Tinctoria is now a textile studio run by Leentje van Hengel. In the long, slender space, linen, wool, silk, hemp, bamboo, velvet (made from silk and viscose), and cotton are dyed with natural plant dyes. For twenty years, Leentje has been mastering this skill in order to make sumptuous textiles for a variety of European clients. She works with interior decorators, organic cotton wholesalers, and fashion designers, as well as private clients—all looking for a unique product.

Leentje screen-prints her fabrics in the atelier—there are dozens of large printing boards leaning against the walls, all with interesting patterns and details. The colors she creates are stunning—muted rose, cherry, cerulean, deep ochre, and soft grass are just a few of my favorites. Although Leentje works mostly on large-scale productions, she also makes home furnishings, such as bedspreads and cushions, to order.

Leaf through her many wonderful sample boards, and select a palette and print that suit your taste. Prices vary greatly depending on what color, fabric, and quantity you order, but for those of us who are interested in beautiful and distinctive textiles for small projects, Leentje always has a cupboard or two full of surplus cuts to choose from. Velvets range from 25€ to 60€ per meter. There is also a large basket full of small pieces of cotton, linen, and silk, which sell for 8.50€ per 100 grams.

WANDER

8

Between Canals

WANDER

8

I MAY BE A LITTLE BIASED BECAUSE THIS IS MY NEIGHBORHOOD, BUT I'M SURE OTHERS AGREE THAT THE *GRACHTENGORDEL ZUID* (THE southern girdle of canals) is one of the most charming quarters of Amsterdam. As I wander through these particular canal streets and gaze up at the unchanged seventeenth-century houses, I always find something utterly delightful—something that inevitably catches my imagination and inspiration. In this wander, I have chosen four hand-made havens that will provide the perfect inspirational stops as you stroll between the canals. And as you wander from place to place, take your time. Stand on a bridge and watch the boats pass by underneath, or take rest on a bench to soak in the old-world atmosphere. Perhaps you will hear the chiming of one of the nearby churches, or the soft bell of a passing bike.

THE FROZEN FOUNTAIN

Prinsengracht 645
TELEPHONE + 31 (0)20 6229375
Monday + 1:00 pm to 6:00 pm
Tuesday through Saturday + 10:00 am to 6:00 pm
Sunday + 1:00 pm to 5:00 pm
www.frozenfountain.nl

THE FROZEN FOUNTAIN IS A DESIGN DESTINATION WHERE MANY NEW CRAFTSPEOPLE AND DESIGNERS FROM THE Netherlands and Europe are presented, thanks to the owners Dick Dankers and Cok de Rooy, who, since the store's inception fifteen years ago, have been scouting Dutch design academies for emerging designers.

The collection at The Frozen Fountain grows weekly, and seems to include everything and anything. Some of my favorite designers are Piet Hein Eek, a woodworker who makes sought-after chairs, tables, and sofas from rescued wood; Hella Jongerius, who uses traditional techniques to create a large line of ceramics; and Claudy Jongstra, who uses the wool from her own sheep for large felt wall hangings and rugs.

This distinguished shop is frequented by both local and international stylists; photographers and design journalists seem to visit daily. It is not out of the ordinary to see a TV cameraman following a presenter, slowly meandering through the store to show viewers the best of the best in European

"THE FLAX PROJECT" by christien meindertsma in conjunction with zuiderzee museum.

design and craft—much of it is exclusive to The Frozen Fountain. What I love most about Frozen Fountain is that the collection is eclectic and wide, and is not just focused on high-end design. The owners' discerning eyes seek not only ambitious young Dutch designers with international aspirations, but also those content to continue working on their own, in their own studio with their own two hands. It's quite unusual in Amsterdam for high design and handmade to be shown together, but The Frozen Fountain is one of the rare places that mixes both, and beautifully so.

GALERIE LOUISE SMIT

Prinsengracht 615
TELEPHONE + 31 (0)20 6259898
Wednesday through Friday + 2:00 pm to 6:00 pm
Saturday + 1:00 pm to 5:00 pm, and by appointment
www.louisesmit.nl

———

JUST AROUND THE CORNER FROM THE FROZEN FOUNTAIN, AND DOWN A FEW STEPS, IS A QUIET CAVE-LIKE DWELLing dedicated to showcasing exclusive contemporary jewelry. Arranged in glass boxes on wooden plinths placed around the room and on the walls are the latest exhibition pieces of a few of the gallery's thirty or so international and local jewelry artists.

Gallery owner and curator Louise Smit, who is married to a jeweler, saw the need for a gallery devoted to a well-curated collection of wearable art. She opened the space in 1986 after teaching modern ballet for many years, and began hosting exhibitions and promoting her artists; the gallery now has an international following.

Louise has an unmatched aesthetic when selecting jewelry artists for her gallery. While I was researching unique and handmade jewelry in Amsterdam, all trails kept leading back to Louise, and I soon realized that she represented almost all the jewelers that I had my eye on for this book. Among my picks—all represented by Louise—are Dutch designer Iris Nieuwenberg, who is currently inspired by eighteenth-century interiors and gardens and assembles brooches, earrings, and necklaces made from images, dollhouse furnishings, and other antique elements; Jacomijn van der Donk, who uses pebbles, twigs, and brushes to create striking necklaces and rings; and Mette Sabye, whose recent exhibition, called "…another man's treasure," displayed pieces made by combining found objects, such as a tiny porcelain teacup or old family banknotes, with exquisite gems.

Louise is welcoming and happy for you to just browse or have a close look at a piece of jewelry that catches your eye. Although pieces start at a luxurious 500€, for lovers of handmade, one-of-a-kind jewelry, this is a place in Amsterdam not to be missed. Her detailed website has more information about each artist, and to join the mailing list for upcoming events and exhibitions (there are eight or so a year), just send her an email or give her a call.

KNOPENWINKEL

Herengracht 389
TELEPHONE + 31 (0)20 6269472
Monday + 1:00 pm to 6:00 pm
Tuesday through Saturday + 11:00 am to 6:00 pm
www.knopenwinkel.net

◆

J UST BEYOND A BEND IN THE HERENGRACHT, SET IN A 1920S CANAL HOUSE, IS A DARLING BOUTIQUE WITH YELLOW-AND-white striped canvas awnings and a giant old-fashioned-style wooden button hanging above the doorway. There is a wooden slat chair or two outside the blue trimmed windows in which to sit and soak in the sun, but you won't linger outside the shop too long—one peek through the window will have you pushing the button doorknob to discover what awaits inside.

Knopenwinkel simply translates as Button Shop, and that is exactly what you will find inside—thousands and thousands of buttons made from all different materials, from all over the world. Thea de Boer is the proprietress and master button acquirer, having spent more than twenty-two years scouting everywhere she travels for the most interesting buttons. While her collection is impressive, so are her hand-made button-inspired home and fashion accessories. She makes beautiful button-covered lampshades that sit on glass bases, necklaces from all sorts of buttons; even the front door open sign is crafted from tiny white buttons stitched onto lush dark velvet. Some of the most exclusive buttons in

her collection are what she calls her "jewels," a huge collection of gem-like buttons from Italy, and others culled from *haute couture* that are at least fifty years old. Thea holds textile and other art exhibitions every six weeks or so in a gallery space at the back of the shop.

The boutique has a distinct Asian accent, with dark wood cabinets and chests from India and silk scarves and wall hangings from other faraway lands creating stylish backdrops. But the shop remains quintessentially old European; paintings by artist Anna Pavlova line the walls, depicting familiar Dutch and French streetscapes, while 1920s-style chandeliers and shelving units, and glass jars filled with buttons, add to the atmosphere of days of long ago.

Buttons range from 10 cents to 20€.

YDU – YOUNG DESIGNERS UNITED

Keizersgracht 447
TELEPHONE + 31 (0)20 6269191
Monday ◆ 1:00 pm to 6:00 pm
Tuesday through Saturday ◆ 10:00 am to 6:00 pm
(Thursday until 8:00 pm)
www.ydu.nl

———◆———

YDU IS MORE THAN A FASHION BOUTIQUE SELLING THE LAT-
EST AND MOST STYLISH READY-TO-WEAR CLOTHES: IT'S A
platform for young fashion designers, a collective point-
of-sale room that not only helps new designers start their
own labels, but also gives clientele a chance to buy affordable and unique garments and fashion accessories from talented emerging designers.

Angelika Groenendijk-Wasylewski is the founder of this
very popular showroom. She launched her business in 2003
after seeing how many of her talented friends—fresh out
of school—didn't have a way to sell their clothing, other
than by taking on the daunting task of starting their own
businesses. Angelika created a place where young designers could translate their creative visions into wearable,
reasonably priced collections. The initiative also provides
guidance, assistance, and feedback to designers while they
develop their labels. Customers are given the opportunity
to buy chic, individually tailored clothes from designers like
Iefke de Roos, who makes all her garments by hand and in
limited editions; Barbara Munsel, who uses only natural and

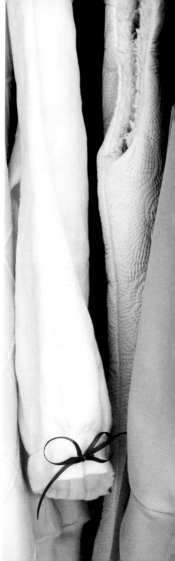

organic materials that she dyes and prints by hand; and Els Petit, who embroiders the fabric she uses to make sophisticated leisurewear. Currently there are fourteen clothing designers and five accessory designers in YDU, all unique and distinct.

Twice a year, during Amsterdam International Fashion week, Angelika organizes an event in the shop when designers and customers can interact. Some of my favorite past events included a workshop where Angelika and the YDU designers invited people to bring in a worn-out, unwearable piece of beloved clothing that the designers would revamp or give a new look within half an hour. This past summer, at the "Dress for less or more" workshop, customers were invited to work with their favorite YDU designer to create a garment. By selecting and buying their own fabric, with the aid of the YDU team, clients could decide how expensive or inexpensive their new garment would be.

Garments average between 70€ and 250€, with some accessories more or less expensive, depending on the item.

WANDER

9

Antique Quarter

ARPHI ANTIQUES & ATELIER

ANNEKE SCHAT

TESSELSCHADE-ARBEID ADELT

WANDER

9

THIS QUARTER OF AMSTERDAM IS ENCHANTING AND MAGICAL, BURST-ING WITH CHARACTER, WOVEN BY THE THREADS OF TIME, WITH THE magnificent and grandfatherly Rijks Museum as its focus. This quarter is the ultimate wanderer's terrain.

I have picked only three special places for this wander because, although there are shops that offer the handmade dotted all over, they are for you to find. Experience the thrill of discovering your own: step off the beaten track, head down quaint little streets that look quiet but alluring in some way, for some reason yet unknown to you. This quarter is filled with just such streets; it's an ideal place to wander in search of ateliers and antiques. If you are in the area for any time at all, you will hear the Rijks bells chiming overhead, which makes the experience all the more atmospheric.

For rest stops, I suggest the tearoom of Chocolaterie Pompadour (Kerkstraat 148), or Soup en Zo (Nieuwe Spiegelstraat 54) for a delicious takeaway homemade soup or salad, or a drink at the old Hans en Grietje café (Spiegelgracht 27). Finally, when you head up to the Leidseplein to visit Tesselschade (see below), take refuge afterward in Café Americain for some Art Nouveau opulence as you sip your beverage of choice. Ah Amsterdam, you know how to make us swoon.

ARPHI ANTIQUES & ATELIER

Prinsengracht 827
TELEPHONE + 31 (0)20 6204074 or + 31 (0)6 14368554
Thursday & Friday ⋆ 11:00 am to 6:00 pm
Saturday ⋆ 11:00 am to 5:00 pm

———◆———

UST OFF THE SPEIGELGRACHT, THE ANCIENT PATH KNOWN AS THE RED CARPET TO THE RIJKS MUSEUM, IS A LITTLE shopfront with a simple old-fashioned iron sign hanging above the door that says "Atelier & Antiques." It is run by longtime interior decorator Odette Welvaars and her daughter, artist Julie Arphi. This quaint-looking boutique is a much-loved stop of mine, as there is always something old that is new in store, something with a rich history and impeccable style.

Odette has been an interior decorator for many years. She has designed and furnished the interiors of homes throughout Europe, and her shop is filled with fabulous antiques that she and business partner Ola Nordström have sourced in Sweden, France, Italy, and Spain, as well as locally. Ola lives in Sweden most of the time and has been sourcing and restoring antiques for eighteen years. He often finds the best pieces well-hidden in forests, literally—in homes that are deep in the Swedish woodlands.

Julie has a studio behind the store, as well as another in a neighboring quarter. Her rich, textural paintings are dispersed throughout the long, narrow store and perfectly

complement the time-layered, richly-patined furniture. Although she often works on a grand scale, painting canvases on commission for large spaces, at the moment she is drawn to painting portraits, some on wallpaper that is more than two hundred years old. She also paints watercolors of fruits and flora.

In the center of the shop is an open kitchen-like area where you may find Julie, Odette, or Ola sipping coffee and chatting with clients or visitors. If you are there to browse, don't hesitate to step around them and wander toward the back of the store, where you will find exquisite chandeliers dangling from a glass ceiling; a table filled with glass domes, bottles, and cake stands; fresh flowers; and handmade ceramics, some old, some newly made by local artists, strewn across every surface. The boutique is arranged like a series of open rooms in a sumptuous, sophisticated home.

ANNEKE SCHAT

Spiegelgracht 20A
TELEPHONE + 31 (0)20 6251608
Thursday & Friday • 10:00 am to 6:00 pm
Saturday • 10:00 am to 5:00 pm, and by appointment
www.annekeschat.nl

M ETAL SCULPTOR, JEWELRY ARTIST, AND PAINTER ANNEKE HAS, FOR FOUR DECADES, DRAWN INSPIRATION FROM THE earth's elements, Japanese calligraphy, and lately, an ever-increasing fascination and observation of the circle.

Anneke likes to work with gold and silver equally, and chooses these metals because of their beauty and connection to the earth, not for their monetary value. When you look close, you can see the detail that has gone into soldering each tiny shard of gold or silver to another, creating complex wearable sculptures.

Anneke works in her atelier above the gallery space, just a moment's stroll from the Rijks Museum. Her pieces start at around 300€ (with most pieces selling for about 1000€ or more).

TESSELSCHADE-ARBEID ADELT

Leidseplein 33
TELEPHONE + 31 (0)20 6236665
Tuesday through Friday • 11:00 am to 5:30 pm
Saturday • 10:00 am to 5:00 pm
www.tesselschade-arbeidadelt.nl

I N THE ALWAYS BUSY AND AT TIMES GRUNGY LEIDSEPLEIN, AMSTERDAM'S ENTERTAINMENT DISTRICT, LIES AN UNEX- pected treasure. Wedged in between a foreign exchange bureau and a florist is a remarkable slice of Dutch history— not a museum or church, but a beautiful old boutique that has been selling articles made by local craftswomen for more than one hundred years. Tesselschade-Arbeid Adelt is a type of co-op that was established in 1871 to support women in their goal of economic independence. Today the Amsterdam boutique is one of six throughout the Netherlands.

The only selection criteria the organization adheres to is that everything made by the members has to be top-quality, so the store is always stocked with beautifully crafted home- wares. Inside, you will find smocked dresses and knitted booties for little ones, tea cozies, embroideries, tablecloths, samplers, sweaters, and many traditional decorations for the home, all made by hand. This is an especially wonderful place to come if you are on the lookout for baby gifts—the range of handcrafted toys, rattles, bibs, and outfits is plentiful. The association is volunteer-based, which keeps the prices very affordable—you can find items in store for just 2€.

WANDER

10

De Pijp

WANDER

10

DE PIJP MAY LOOK LIKE A RATHER HECTIC AND OFTEN CROWDED NEIGHBORHOOD, ESPECIALLY IF YOU HEAD STRAIGHT TO THE BUStling Albert Cuyp market. But if you meander off the well-trodden main *straat*, you will find many beautiful tree-lined thoroughfares, calm and picturesque, dotted with delightful restaurants, specialty stores, and hidden ateliers. This is a culturally diverse and highly creative area where you will want to stop and smell the roses; take time to soak in the atmosphere, and end your wander by dining in one of the restaurants on the ever-charming Frans Halstraat. I recommend each and every restaurant, although my favorites are De Witte Uyl (The White Owl, Frans Halsstraat 26), De Drie Vrienden (The Three Friends, Frans Halsstraat 28), and Más Tapas (Saenredamstraat 37 hs) for fabulous Spanish tapas.

ATELIER TEMPEL

Eerste Jacob van Campenstraat 20 hs
TELEPHONE + 31 (0)20 4700106
Most weekdays · 11:00 am to 6:00 pm (best to call first)
www.ateliertempel.nl

❖

ILDE TEMPELMAN'S QUAINT SHOPFRONT IS FILLED WITH HAND-PAINTED PLATTERS, EMBROIDERED BAGS, PLUMP little painted teapots, and hanging ornaments displayed beautifully in rows of shelves. The display is like a storyboard that I found myself reading visually from left to right, then right to left, going on an imaginative journey under the sea, through a forest, and inside an elegant home filled with chandeliers and such, all drawn by the hands of one gifted artist.

Hilde, who has a background in fashion and textiles, worked for many years as a children's-wear designer with companies including Oilily. She decided to branch out on her own almost fifteen years ago, first buying an old greengrocer store, then converting it into her studio and home. Her love of working with textiles remains strong—she still freelances for various fashion houses—but ceramics have become her central passion.

When you first step into the tiny space behind the window, you'll notice a kiln, which is fired up whenever Hilde has a new collection ready. She also screen-prints ceramics, and says she loves the combination of hand-drawn illustrations with

photographic-like transfers: "I like to draw on everything, I can't help decorating things," she explains. Hilde also finds vintage platters and adds her illustrations or screen prints to them, enhancing each piece and giving it a new life.

Tempelman's inspiration comes from classic paintings and the interiors of old houses; she loves to visit ancient castles and gardens. She is also inspired by Dutch folk dress. As a child, she adored the intricate outfits worn by traditional Dutch women, and made her own garments based on them. *De kraakheldere boerin*, which roughly translates as "the crispy clean farm woman," is a Dutch icon that recurs repeatedly throughout her work. Hilde screen-prints depictions of farm women on postcards, porcelain ware, brooches, and buttons.

Her eclectic collection is a kitschy modern take on the traditional Dutch style. Small hand-painted plates which she calls "dishes with wishes" cost around 12€ to 15€ each, and large platters around 200€. Teapots range from 65€ to 85€.

KERAMIEK VAN CAMPEN

Eerste Jacob van Campenstraat 38 hs
TELEPHONE + 31 (0)20 4194390 or + 31 (0)6 29130883
Daily from 11:00 am (best to call first)
www.keramiekvancampen.nl

❖

WHEN I FIRST MOVED TO AMSTERDAM, I SPENT MANY AN EVENING PEERING THROUGH THE WINDOWS OF THIS charming atelier and boutique while walking home after dining in one of the restaurants on Frans Halsstraat. I was forever intrigued by the new clay works on display and was so smitten with the light-filled, uncomplicated space that I often fancied joining one of the ceramics workshops advertised on the front door.

Keramiek van Campen is run by three local ceramicists—Andrea Boerman, Inge van Bogerijen, and Floor Toot. There is something about their work that, simply said, ignites and delights. While Inge's work is abstract, Floor creates very traditional French pottery on the wheel, making practical wares such as jugs, bowls, and cups. Andrea's is Escher-inspired, with repeating patterns of shapes and fanciful creatures.

Among the objects created by the three are highly sculptural vases, platters, and urns; light shades; wearable ceramics; and even large decorative rock forms and stone towers. The creations are diverse, and the designs are always evolving. Although from the outside, the space looks more like an

atelier than a boutique, all pieces on display in the front room are for sale, and you are more than welcome to take your time and browse. Prices start at 10€, with cups and bowls averaging 20€ to 50€. Day-long workshops are held in which students work with each artisan to create, by the end of the session, three unique pieces.

HAPPY RED FISH
HAGAR VARDIMON

Eerste Jacob van Campenstraat 44 hs
TELEPHONE + 31 (0)20 6736621
Open by appointment
www.happy-red-fish.com

TEXTILE AND SOFT SCULPTURE MAKER HAGAR VARDIMON LIVES AND WORKS JUST A FEW STEPS PAST KERAMIEK VAN Campen. Hagar, originally from Israel and married to a Dutchman, established her home and atelier in what used to be, a century or so ago, a neighborhood herb and tea store. Today, the front room is a display area for her thread illustrations, soft sculpture chairs, whales, and Luna dolls.

Hagar studied art and spent many years painting large-scale canvases, but now makes soft sculptures with needle, thread, and ink on cotton. Each Luna doll is a simple, imaginary girl, always dressed in an Edwardian outfit, with an emphasis on her facial expression. The Luna series of cute soft sculptures in all different shapes and sizes are all hand-drawn and handmade by Hagar. Prices for Luna dolls range from 20€ to 45€. Textile creations and thread art range from 10€ to 200€. Commissions for larger pieces are accepted, and international shipping is available. Although usually only open to the public once a year during the open atelier weekends, Hagar is happy to have visitors interested in her work stop by, so don't hesitate to ring the doorbell.

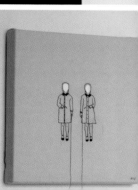

WERKPLAATS WILLEMIEN

2e Jacob van Campenstraat 2
TELEPHONE + 31 (0)20 6646308
Tuesday through Friday + 10:00 am to 6:00 pm
Saturday + 11:00 am to 5:00 pm
www.werkplaatswillemien.nl

T UCKED BEHIND THE ORIGINAL HEINEKEN BREWERY ON THE SECOND JACOB VAN CAMPENSTRAAT IS A HUMBLE but quaint little corner store filled with pretty screen-printed linens, handmade ceramic teapots, stools covered with stitched leather and feathers, hand-embroidered cushions, illustrated plates and tableware, beautiful upholstery fabrics, and…lots of chairs. This is the workplace of upholsterer and shop owner Willemien Westenenk, who collaborates with local craftspeople to create sophisticated and highly sought-after furnishings.

Willemien adores chairs and has been an upholsterer most of her life. Her studio adjoins the storefront where commissioned pieces constantly go in and out of the shop's Dutch doors. Screen-printed fabric and teapots made with the ancient Japanese technique Bankoyaki, by Haruka Matsuo, a Japanese designer based in the Netherlands, are scattered around the boutique, mixing beautifully with Willemien's exceptional upholstery work. Willemien has created a lovely oasis of pretty florals and ethnic-inspired homewares amongst the busy streets of De Pijp, a fabulous place to find handmade treasures crafted by local artisans.

DEPSTER

Govert Flinckstraat 219
TELEPHONE + 31 (0)6 20203085
Open most weekdays, call for an appointment

◆

EPSTER IS ALMOST CERTAINLY AMSTERDAM'S BEST-KEPT HANDMADE SHOPPING SECRET. THE FIRST TIME I DIScovered this inconspicuous little studio was during an open atelier weekend in De Pijp. The space was bursting with happy customers who had purchased a number of designer Margriet Deppe's handmade luxury leather bags over the years. The studio is set in her own home on a street parallel to the famous Albert Cuyp market.

With more than twenty styles to choose from, Margriet invites you to come in and select a leather, a lining fabric, and the trimmings for your one-of-a-kind bag. A visit to the studio is the best way to see all the leathers on offer and get a feel for the right bag. Her creations are of exceptional quality, and her designs are modern and sophisticated. My favorites in her collection are the "ladies traveler" bag (with a clever compartment in the bottom for carrying overnight stay garments) and the "leather chic" and "Paris" bags, complete with fringe and Italian bronze- or gold-plated rings and buckles. Clutches start at 99€ and handbags are priced from 250€ to 399€.

AUTHOR'S FAVORITES

INDEX

Pia Jane Bijkerk is an Australian stylist and photographer specializing in still life, food, interiors, and lifestyle imagery. She is the author of *Paris: Made by Hand* (The Little Bookroom). Pia lives in Amsterdam and Paris, and works internationally for magazines and advertising agencies. As a stylist she has worked around the world for clients including *Vogue Entertaining + Travel*, *Gourmet Traveller*, *Real Simple*, Saatchi and Saatchi, Tommy Hilfiger and Philips. Her work can be seen at piajanebijkerk.com.